nen

enneko nen

eia tuia

bua bua

ea la ea

yo yo

abua

arror

hush baby hush

bayoo bayooshki arror

ea la e

lalo lalo

bayoo

yo yo yo yo

tulla lu lu yo

hushabye

dan

tulla

duermete

dandini

arroro

lullay

For my mother who sang to us,
for my children who listened in their turn
and for everyone everywhere with a baby in their arms – *KH*

For my beautiful Mila Maisie – *PS*

Hush, Baby, Hush!

Lullabies from around the World

I would like to thank everyone who helped me gather lullabies for this book, including:
Bryce Anderson, Frankie Armstrong, Elin Bolsø, Ingrid Bolsø Berdal, Juliana Bayfield,
the staff of the British Library and Sound Archive, Ruth Carneson, Mircan Caya, Hyechong Chung,
Phillippa Clayden, Nick Davidson, Mehmet Ali Dikerdem, Brita Granstrom,
Lamia al-Gailani Werr and Azza al-Gailani, Fran Hazelton, Keiko Holt, Mehiyar Kathem of Culture for All, Baghdad,
Zohreh Korangi, Sam Lee, Tony, Sue and Imi Maufe, Gill Millar, Davia Nelson and The Kitchen Sisters,
Keishi Nagatsuka, Ece Ozdemiroglu, Joe O'Connor, Erika Pál, Lefteris Panteli, Elena Logara Panteli, Aili Pello,
Edda Peris and her mother Armida Sgnaolin, Yelena Pershina , Jim Riordan, Narmin Rasizade, Heike Schmidt, John Shave,
Allama Siddiki, Deputy High Commissioner at the Bangladesh High Commission in London and his wife and colleagues,
Sidsel Sørenson, Marina Tafur, Nick Thorpe, Shanti Venkatesh and Divya Mathur at the Nehru Centre, London,
Peta Webb at Cecil Sharp House Library, Andrea Weizinger, Albrecht Wiedmann,
Sunghee Yu and her mother, Byungyun Kim. KH

JANETTA OTTER-BARRY BOOKS

This selection and English translations copyright © Kathy Henderson 2010 except for
'Wampanoag Lullaby' copyright © Manitonquat 1994,
'Alulu' text and music copyright © Dorothy Berliner Commins 1967,
'Maranoa Lullaby' English text copyright © Mark Leehy and Kevin O'Mara 1993.
Illustrations copyright © Pam Smy 2010
Musical transcriptions by Dave King, Sound World (www.akabella.net)

First published in Great Britain in 2010 and in the USA in 2011 by
Frances Lincoln Children's Books, 4 Torriano Mews,
Torriano Avenue, London NW5 2RZ
www.franceslincoln.com

A catalogue record for this book is available from the British Library
ISBN: 978-1-84507-967-3

Illustrated with with oil paint and coloured pencils with linework on acetate overlays
Set in ITC Stone Serif and Sans Serif
Printed in Dongguan, Guangdong, China by Toppan Leefung in July 2010

1 3 5 7 9 8 6 4 2

Hush, Baby, Hush!

Lullabies from around the World

Kathy Henderson
Illustrated by Pam Smy

F

FRANCES LINCOLN
CHILDREN'S BOOKS

Contents

Introduction

Lullabies are remarkable. All round the world, for as long as babies have fretted and carers have coped, ordinary people have made up these songs on the spot, passed them on by word of mouth from one generation to another and sometimes written them down.

This is a small collection of lullabies from the oral traditions of the world. In them, like flies in amber, are glimpses of other people's lives and feelings and ways of caring. Are you pacing the floor in the middle of the night with a restless child? One look at this collection and you know you're not alone, that what you're doing is what people everywhere have always done. Lullabies connect us across cultures and through time in a universal poetry.

Nor are these only songs for bedtime. Just as babies fret at different times of day, wake and sleep or cry and cry at any time for a hundred different, unknowable reasons, so there are lullabies of all kinds - loving, laughing, cajoling, soothing, irritable, threatening, fantastical - just like us. Lullabies run the whole range of emotions from celebration to desperation. They're what we do when words and reasoning don't work.

These are songs which face two ways at once. They soothe the baby but, equally important, they relieve the carer. Today's experts advise us to switch on the calming sound of the vacuum cleaner and leave the room or phone a helpline before we lose our temper with a persistently crying baby. Lullabies got there first. In their tunes, rhythms and the sound patterns of their words they're repetitive, calming, soothing for the child. But in the act of singing and very often in what they say they relieve the feelings of the harassed carer.

This collection brings together lullabies from many different languages and cultures and offers a glimpse of a world that holds babies in its arms and does its best.

The songs are presented in their original language (where scripts differ they are transcribed phonetically) with translations beside them, and there's music for many of them at the back of the book. I hope that, like the people who made them you will go on adapting them, put your own children's names in, make them your own and pass them on.

K Henderson

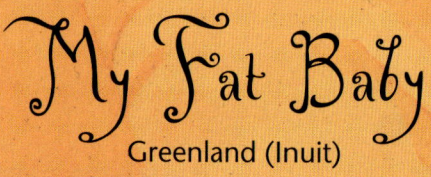

My Fat Baby

Greenland (Inuit)

It's my fat baby
I feel in my hood,
Oh how heavy he is!
Ya ya! Ya ya!

When I turn my head
He smiles at me, my baby,
Hidden deep in my hood,
Oh how heavy he is!
Ya ya! Ya ya!

How pretty he is when he smiles
With his two teeth, like a little walrus!
Oh I'd rather my baby were heavy,
So long as my hood is full!

Heart-finder
North America (Wampanoag)

Wunny wunny krietta

Tashinahanu

Wunny Wamiaquene

Wunnitu Tahnam

Beautiful beautiful bundle

The wind laughs

All is peace and beauty

Beautiful heart-finder

13

Black-Eyed Peas with Onions
Turkey

Ninni de ninni ninnice,
Bol soğanlı börülce,
Yesin benim oğlum doyunca,
Mini mini yavrum ninni.

Dandini dandini dan, ister
Bey babasından don ister
Basmadan beğenmez oğlum
Kadifeden don ister.

Lullaby lullaby lullaby,
Black-eyed peas with onions,
Let my son eat till he's full,
Lullaby lullaby lullaby.

Dandini dandini dan, he wants
Trousers from his father has,
He doesn't like the cotton ones,
Soft as velvet's what he wants.

Candy Floss
Iraq

Nishteri yakhouti yallah
Banat sha'ar
Abat wein awalli wein?
Banat sha'ar
Bildarbounah abat
Banat sha'ar
illaila 'dna bat bazounah
tkharnushak la la
Banat sha'ar

Come on, friends, let's go shopping for
Candy floss
Where shall I go, where shall I sleep?
Candy floss
I'll sleep in the alleyway.
Candy floss
Don't do that, the cat will scratch you!
You stay here with us tonight.
Candy floss

This is a call and answer song: the children sing the refrain.

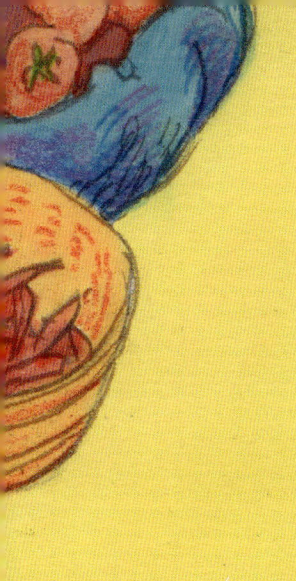

Stir, Stir the Chocolate!

Mexico

Bate, bate chocolate!
Tu nariz de cacahuate.
   Uno, dos, tres, CHO!
   Uno, dos, tres, CO!
   Uno, dos, tres, LA!
   Uno, dos, tres, TE!
Chocolate, chocolate!
Bate, bate chocolate!
Bate, bate, bate, bate,
Bate, bate CHOCOLATE!

Stir, stir the chocolate!
Your nose is like a peanut.
   One, two, three, CHO!
   One, two, three, CO!
   One, two, three, LA!
   One, two, three, TE!
Chocolate, chocolate!
Stir, stir the chocolate!
Stir, stir, stir, stir,
Stir, stir the CHOCOLATE!

In Mexico hot chocolate is made with a whisk that's twirled between the palms
of your hands, so rub your hands in time with the words as you say this rhyme.

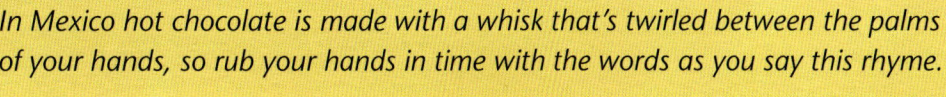

Sugar, Bread and Butter

India (Hindi)

Neeni baba neeni,
Muchan, roti, cheeni,
Muchan, roti hoghia,
Mayrah baba soghia.

Hush my baby, hush-a,
Sugar, bread and butter,
The sugar bread's all eaten,
My baby should be sleeping.

15

Oh My Child

Nigeria (Yoruba)

Omo o ee npe dagba
  Omo o ee npe dagba
Kekere jojolo ma bi temi o
  Omo o ee npe dagba.

Kekere jojolo ma bi temi o
  Omo o ee npe dagba
Bomo mi dagba a di loya o
  Omo o ee npe dagba
Bomo mi dagba adi doctor o
  Omo o ee npe dagba
Bomo mi dagba a sorire
  Omo o ee npe dagba.

Omo o ee npe dagba
Kekere jojolo ma bi temi o
  Omo o ee npe dagba
Kekere jojolo ma bi temi o
  Omo o ee npe dagba.

Oh my child, you're growing up so fast,
  Oh my child, you're growing up so fast.
You, my sweet and lovely baby,
  Oh my child, you're growing up so fast.

You, my sweet and lovely baby,
  Oh my child, you're growing up so fast.
When you grow up, child, may you be a lawyer,
  Oh my child, you're growing up so fast.
When you grow up, child, may you be a doctor,
  Oh my child, you're growing up so fast.
When you grow up, child, may you be lucky,
  Oh my child, you're growing up so fast.

Oh my child, you're growing up so fast.
You, my sweet and lovely baby,
Oh my child, you're growing up so fast.
You, my sweet and lovely baby,
Oh my child, you're growing up so fast.

Row, Row to the Fishing Rock

Norway

Ro, ro til fiskekjaer,
Mange fisker får vi der.
En til far og en til mor,
En til søster og en til bror,
Og to til den som fisken dro
Og det var vesle Immi.

Row, row to the fishing rock,
We'll catch many fishes there.
One for Father, one for Mother,
One for your sister and one for your brother,
And two for the one who caught the fish
And that was little Immi.

Smuggler's Lullaby

Wales

Hush-a-bye baby, down by the sea,
The ship is a-waiting for you and for me,
For you and for me.

To take us to Bristol or Barnstaple Bay,
Where prizes are for us by night and by day,
By night and by day.

17

Alulu

Malawi

Alulu, alulu, alulu mwana.
Dumadzi ndinkanaye.
Kunkhuni ndinkanaye.
Kumunda ndinkanaye.
Pophika sendera uko,
Mwana wamwini,
Ndingakutente
Kulongolola kulipatali.
Alulu.

Hush, hush, hush child.
When I go for water, the child is on my back.
When I go for firewood, the child is on my back.
When I go to the fields, the child is on my back.
When I cook, move away, over there,
Child of someone else,
Or I might burn you
And that would make them grumble for a long time.
Hush.

18

Go to Sleep

Spain

Duermete mi niño,
Duermete mi sol,
Duermete pedazo de mi corazón.

    0-0 0-0 0-0 0
    0-0 0-0 0

Duermete mi niño,
Que tengo que hacer,
Lavar los pañuelos planchar y coser.

    0-0 0-0 0-0 0 . . .

Duermete mi niño,
Duermete solito,
Que cuando despiertes,
Te daró atolito.

    0-0 0-0 0-0 0 . . .

Go to sleep my baby,
Go to sleep sunshine,
Go to sleep you piece of this heart of mine.

Go to sleep my baby,
I've got things to do,
Handkerchiefs to wash and to iron and to sew.

Go to sleep my baby,
Sleep all on your own,
And when you wake
You'll have soup made of corn.

19

Hush Baby Hush

Jamaica

Hush baby hush,
　　Mama's gonna market fe buy Coca Cola.
Hush lady hush,
　　Fe Mama's gonna market fe buy Coca Cola,
　　Papa's gonna bush fe go look the wood,
　　So Mama soon come with sweet sweet candy,
　　Mama soon come with the sweet sweet candy,
Hush baby hush,
　　Pass the nipple bottle, let me give you feedin so,
Hush lady hush,
　　Gimme little bottle, let me give you feedin so,
Hush baby hush.

Hush baby hush,
　　Se mama's gonna market fe buy Coca Cola,
　　Papa gonna bush fe go look up the wood,
　　Catch up the fire, put on the pot,
　　The Mama come back, your belly will be full.
　Hush baby hush,
　　Mama's gonna market,
Hush lady hush.

Sleep, Sleep, Little One

Japan

Nen nen kororiyo okororiyo
Boya wa yoikoda nenne shina.

Boya no omori wa doko e itta
Ano yama koete sato e itta.

Sato no miyage ni nani morota
Dendentaiko ni sho no fue.

Sleep, sleep, little one rocking there,
Be a good baby and go to sleep.

Where's your nurse gone, little baby?
Home to her village far over the mountain.

What will she bring you from her village?
A rat-a-tat drum and a whistle too.

22

Ja-Jangka

Korea

Ja-jang, ja-jang woori aga
Woori aga jaldo janda.

Koko dalga wooji mara
Woori aegi jamul gella
Mony geya wooji mara
Woori aegi jamul gella.

Kumul jundll nawul sari
Eunul jundll nawul saari
Kumja Donga, eunja donga
Hanll gatn bobae donga
Ja-jang, ja-jang woori aga
Woori aga jaldo janda.

Ja-jang, ja-jang, my little baby.
Little baby, sleep well, sleep well.

Rooster, Cockadoodle doo,
Don't crow and wake the baby up.
Dog, don't bark that Woof Woof Woof!
Or you'll wake the baby up.

I wouldn't change you for sacks of gold,
I wouldn't change you for stacks of silver,
My golden child, my silver child,
You are as precious as the sky.
Pat-pat, pat-pat, my little baby,
Little baby, sleep well, sleep well.

This is a spoken lullaby, with a very strong rhythm as you pat the baby.

23

All the Pretty Little Horses
USA

Hush-a-bye, don't you cry,
Go to sleep my little baby;
When you wake, you shall have
All the pretty little horses.

　Blacks and bays, dapple greys,
　Coach and six little horses.

Way down yonder in the meadow
Poor little baby cries 'Mama'.
Birds and butterflies flutter round his eyes,
Poor little baby cries 'Mama'.

Hush-a-bye, don't you cry,
Go to sleep my little baby;
When you wake, you shall have
All the pretty little horses.

　Blacks and bays, dapple greys,
　Coach and six little horses.

*This is the song of a black slave forced to leave her own baby
down 'in the meadow' so she can look after her master's child.*

24

Sleep, Johnny, Sleep

Czech/Moravian

Spi, Janíčku, spi	Sleep, Johnny, sleep,
Dám ti jabka tři.	I'll give you three apples.
Jedno bude červené,	The first one's a red one,
A to druhé selené.	The second one's a green one.
Spi, Janíčku, spi,	Sleep, Johnny, sleep,
Očička zamži.	Close your little eyes.
Spi Janíčku, spi,	Sleep, Johnny, sleep,
Dám ti jabka tři.	I'll give you three apples.
Jedno bude červené,	The first one's a red one.
A to druhé selené,	The second one's a green one,
A to třetí modré.	The third one's a blue one.
Spi, Janku, dobré.	Dear Johnny, go to sleep.

Go to Bed Tom
UK

Go to bed Tom,
Go to bed Tom,
Tired or not, Tom,
Go to bed Tom!

The Sun Goes Down
Austria (Tirol)

Sunne geht unter,
Mune geht auf,
Gitsch geht schlafen,
Buibn bleibn auf.

The sun goes down,
The moon comes up,
The girl's gone to sleep,
The boys are wide awake.

Bedtime Aunties

Bangladesh

Ghumparani mashi pishi,	Bedtime Aunties, Bedtime Aunties,
Moder bari esho.	Won't you come to our house, please!
Dudh debo, bhat debo,	I'll give you milk, I'll give you rice,
Pet vore keyo.	Eat, eat as much as you like.
Bata vora pan debo,	Here's a box of betel leaves,
Gal vore dheyo.	Chew until your cheeks are full.
Babu-r chokhe ghum nai,	There's no sign of sleep in the little one's eyes,
Ghum diye jeo.	Please get him to sleep before you go.

A 'Mashi' is a maternal aunt and a 'Pishi' is a paternal aunt and in Bangladesh they have the task of getting the childen to go to sleep.

27

Not Luisa!

Italy

Nanna putei,
Tutti i putei fa nanna,
E Luisa no!

E dormi, dormi,
Dormi per un anno.
La sanità a to padre
Poi il guadagno.

La mamma è andata a messa,
Che cosa porta a casa?
Un bel pometo coto
E a Luisa el rosegoto.

Nanna putei,
Tutti i putei fa nanna,
E Luisa no!

Nanna putei,
All the children are asleep,
But not Luisa!

Sleep, sleep,
Sleep for a year.
Good health to your father
And lots of money too.

Mother's gone to mass,
What will she bring home?
A lovely baked apple
And Luisa shall have the core.

Nanna putei,
All the children are asleep,
But not Luisa!

Sleep Come Quickly

France

Sommeil vite, vite, vite,
Sommeil vite, reviens donc!
Nos petits n'veul' pas dormir,
Le sommeil ne veut pas v'nir.
Sommeil vite, vite, vite,
Sommeil endors nos poupons.

Sommeil vite, vite, vite,
Sommeil vite, reviens donc!
Le garçon ouvre ses yeux,
Notre fill' ne vaut pas mieux
Sommeil vite, vite, vite,
Sommeil endors nos poupons.

Sleep come quickly, quickly, quickly,
Sleep come quickly, come here now!
Our little ones won't settle down,
Sleep just doesn't want to come,
Sleep come quickly, quickly, quickly,
Make our darlings go to sleep.

Sleep come quickly, quickly, quickly,
Sleep come quickly, come back now!
The boy lies there with open eyes,
The girl's the same, what a surprise!
Sleep come quickly, quickly, quickly,
Make our darlings go to sleep.

Hushabye, Baby, Hush

Russia

Bayoo, bayooshki, bayoo,
Nye lozheesya na krayoo,
Preedyot serenky volchok,
Tebya skhvateet za bochok.
Eee ootashcheet vo lesok,
Pod rakeetovy koostok;
Tam pteechkee poyoot,
Tebye spat nye dadoot.

Hushabye, baby, hush,
Don't make such a noise
Or the little grey wolf will come
And carry you away.
He'll drag you off into the wood,
Leave you under a hazelnut tree,
And there the birds will sing so loud
You'll never get to sleep at all.

Ninna Nanna

Italy

Ninna nanna, ninna-o
Questo bimbo a chi lo do?

Lo daremo alla Befana
Che lo tiene una settimana!
    Ninna nanna, ninna-o . . .

Lo daremo al lupo nero
Che lo tiene un anno intero!
    Ninna nanna, ninna-o . . .

Lo daremo alla sua Mamma
Che le fa la ninna nanna.
    Ninna nanna, ninna-o . . .

Ninna nanna ninna noo,
Who shall we give the baby to?

Let's give him to the witch Befana
And she'll keep him for a week!
    Ninna nanna ninna noo . . .

Let's give him to the big bad wolf
And he'll keep him for a year!
    Ninna nanna ninna noo . . .

Let's give him to his very own mamma
So she can sing him Ninna nanna.
    Ninna nanna ninna noo . . .

Tutu Maramba

Brazil

Tutu Maramba, não venha mais cá
Que o pai do menino te manda matar.
Bicho papâo, sai de cima do telhado,
Deixa o menino dormir sossegado.

Tutu Maramba, don't come here any more
Or my child's father will drive you from the door.
Get off the roof, you hungry beast
And leave the boy to sleep in peace.

Tutu Maramba is a scary night monster in Brazil.

Sleep, Baby, Sleep

Hungary

Aludj, baba, aludjál,
Feljött már az esti csillag.
Csöngettyűs kis fehér bárány
Hazafelé ballag.
Fészkére szállt az erdőn
A dalos madárka,
Doromboló cicánk
Is felült a patkára.
Aludj, baba, aludjál,
Feljött már az esti csillag,
Csöngettyűs kis fehér bárány
Hazafelé ballag.

Sleep baby, sleep,
The evening star has come,
The little lamb with the tinkling bell
Is slowly heading home.
The smallest of the singing birds
Has flown back to her nest.
The cat has curled up by the fire
To get a bit of rest.
So sleep, baby, sleep,
The evening star has come,
And the little lamb with the tinkling bell
Is slowly heading home.

33

La-La-La Lai

Iran

Gonjeshk la-la,
Sanjab la-la,
Amad dobareh
Mahtab la-la.

Sparrow, sleep now,
Squirrel, sleep now,
The moon's shining high
In the sky again.

La-la-la lai, la-laa la-lai
La-la-la lai, la-laa la-lai
La-la-la lai, la-laa la-lai
La-la-la lai, la-laa la-lai

Goldoon khabeed
Mesleh hameeshe,
Goorbageh saket,
Khabeeded beeshe

The flower's gone to sleep
Like it always does,
Hush now, frog,
The pond is sleeping.

La-la-la lai, la-laa la-lai …

34

Maranoa Lullaby

Australia (Aboriginal)

Mumma warrunno
Murra wathunno
Mumma warrunno
Murra wathunno.

By the firelight,
In the dark of night,
Child against my breast,
Safely you shall rest.

36

Great Grandma's Lullaby

Korea

Saenun, saenun, nung-ge jago,
Gnun gnun gung-ge jago,
Eojae on saekak sinun shin rang
Pumae jamul janda.

The bird is sleeping on a branch,
The mouse is sleeping in its hole,
The bride is sleeping
In her husband's arms.

The Sun Sleeps

Greece

Keemate o eelios sta vouna,
Ee pertheekes sta plagia,
Keemate ke to teknon mou
Me teen hreesee tou mana.

The sun sleeps on the hills,
The partridges on the hillsides,
And my child sleeps too,
With his golden mother.

Black-Eyed Peas with Onions

page 14

Ni – nni de ni – nni ni – n – ni – ce, Bol so – gan – li bö – rül – ce –

Ye -sin be – im o -glum do – yun — ca — Mi – ni mi – ni ya – vrum nin — ni –

Sugar, Bread and Butter

page 15

Nee — ni ba – ba nee — ni, Mu – chan, ro – ti, chee – ni,

Mu – chan, ro – ti ho – ghi – a, May – rah ba – ba so – ghi – a.

Row, Row to the Fishing Rock

page 17

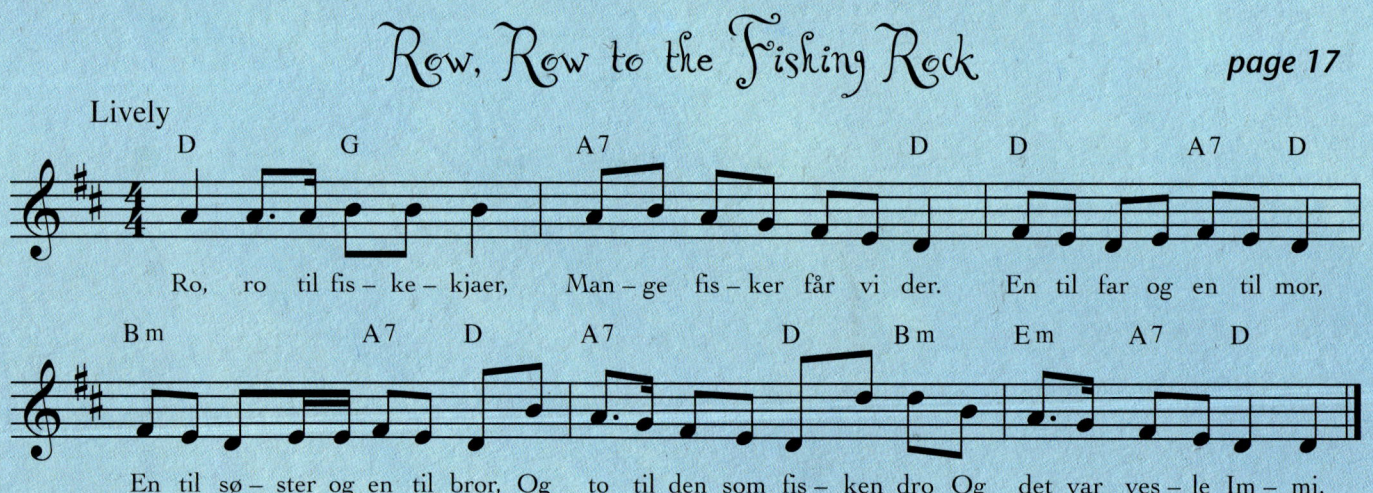

Ro, ro til fis – ke – kjaer, Man – ge fis – ker får vi der. En til far og en til mor,

En til sø – ster og en til bror, Og to til den som fis – ken dro Og det var ves – le Im – mi.

38

Alulu

page 18

Gently

A – lu – lu, a – lu – lu, a – lu – lu mwa – na. Du – mad – zi ndin – ka – na – ye.

Kun – khu – ni ndin – ka – na – ye. Ku – mun – da ndin – ka – na – ye. Po – phi – ka sen – de – ra u – ko,

Mwa – na wam – wi – ni N – din – ga – ku – ten – te Ku – lon – go – lo – la ku – li – pa ta – li. A – lu – lu – lu.

Go To Sleep

page 19

Peacefully

Duer – me – te mi ni – ño –, Duer – me – te mi sol, Duer – me – te pe – da – zo de

mi co – ra – zón o — o — o — o o — o — o

Hush Baby Hush

page 20

With a swing

Hush ba — by hush Ma – ma's go – nna mar – ket fe buy Co – ca Co – la

Hush la – dy hush Fe Ma – ma's go – nna mar – ket fe buy Co – ca Co – la

Pa – pa's go – nna bush fe go look the wood So Ma – ma soon come with sweet sweet can – dy

Sleep, Sleep Little One

page 22

Soothing

Nen ne – n ko – ro – ri – yo o – ko – ro – ri – yo ——

Bo — ya wa yo – i – ko – da nen — ne shi – na.

All the Pretty Little Horses

page 24

Lilting

Dm   C   Am   Dm

Hush – a – bye, don't you cry, Go to sleep my li – ttle ba – by;

Dm   C   Am   Dm

When you wake, you shall have All the pre – tty li – ttle hor – ses.

Am   Dm   Am   Dm

Blacks and bays, da – pple greys, Coach and six — li – ttle - hor ses

Sleep, Johnny, Sleep

page 25

Calmly

C   G7   C   C   G7   C   C   E/B   Am   G

Spi, Ja – ní – cku, spi Dám ti jab – ka tri. Je – dno bu – de cer – ve – né,

C   E/B   Am   G   C   C#°   Dm   G7   C

A to dru – hé ze – le – né. Spi, Ja – ní – cku, spi, O ci – cka zam – zi.

Bedtime Aunties

page 27

Lively

Ghum – pa – ra – ni ma – shi pi – shi, Mo – der ba – ri e – sho. Dudh de – bo, bhat – de – bo,

Pet – vo – re ke – yo. Ba – ta vo – ra pan de – bo, Gal – vo – re dhe – yo.

Slower

Ba – bur cho – khe ghum – nai – Ghum – di – ye je o.

Sleep Come Quickly

page 29

Sweetly

| C | Am | G | C | Am | F | G7 |

Som – meil vi – te, vi – te, vi – te, Som – meil vi – te re – viens donc!

| G | C | F | G | C |

Nos pe – tits n'veul' pas dor – mir, Le som – meil ne veut pas v'nir.

| C | Am | G | C | Am | G | C |

Som – meil vi – te, vi – te, vi – te, Som – meil en – dors nos pou – pons.

Hushabye, Baby, Hush

page 30

Lightly

Ba – yoo, ba – yoo – shki, ba – yoo, Nye lo –zhee –sya na kra – yoo Pree –dyot se –ren –ky vol –chok,

Te – bya skhva –teet za bo –chok Eee oo – tash –cheet vo le –sok, Pod ra –kee – to –vy koo –stok;

Tam pteech – kee po – yoot, Te – bye spat nye da –doot.

Tutu Maramba

page 31

Stately

Tu – tu Ma –ram – ba, não ven – ha mais cá Que o pai do me – ni – no te man – da ma –tar. Bi –

cho pa –pão, sai de ci – ma do tel –ha –do, Dei – xa o me –ni – no dor – mir so –sse – ga –do.

Sleep, Baby, Sleep

page 32

Gently

A – ludj, ba – ba, a – lud – jál, Le – szállt már a csil – lag.

Csön – get – tyüs kis fe – hér bá – rány Ha – za – fe – lé bal – lag.

42

La-La-La Lai

page 34

Maranoa Lullaby

page 36

The Sun Sleeps

page 37

43

LULLABY SOURCE NOTES

Lullabies live in all sorts of places: in families, among friends, in the park, on the street, in books, CDs, radio, TV and the wonderful resources of the internet. They are part of an oral tradition which belongs to all of us. Where the lullabies in this book come from a particular source it is listed below. With many thanks to everyone who sang and wrote and spoke to me and helped me with languages I didn't know. KH

My Fat Baby In *The Unwritten Song*, Vol 1, Willard R Trask , Macmillan, New York 1966. **Heart Finder** Traditional First Nations, USA. copyright © Manitonquat 1994, in *Skip across the Ocean*, Floella Benjamin, Frances Lincoln 1996; **Black-eyed Peas and Onions** Traditional Turkish. On Mircan Caya's CD *Bizim Ninniler*, Can Müzik 2004. English version KH 2010, with thanks to Ece Ozmiroglu; **Candy Floss** Traditional Iraqi lullaby. From Azza and Lamia al Gailani Werr. English version KH 2010; **Stir, Stir the Chocolate!** Traditional Mexican. Many sources including websites and books. English version KH 2010; **Sugar Bread and Butter** Traditional Hindi lullaby. From Gill Millar, Australia. English version KH 2010; **Oh My Child, You're Growing Up So Fast** Traditional Yoruba lullaby from Nigeria. On CD African Lullaby Ellipsis Arts; English version KH 2010; **Row Row to the Fishing Rock** Trad. Norwegian. From Imi Maufe and Frodo Røynesdal. English version KH 2010; **Smuggler's Lullaby** 'Orally gathered by Marie Trevelyan in the Vale of Glamorgan.' In *Lullabies of the Four Nations*, ed Gosset, London, De la More Press, 1915. **Alulu** A lullaby of the Cewa people, a sub-tribe of the Maravi, who live around lake Malawi. In *Lullabies of the World*, Dorothy Berliner Commins, Random House, 1967. **Go To Sleep** Traditional Spanish/ South American. Many sources and variations. English version KH 2010; **Hush Baby Hush** recorded in the 1980s by Davia Nelson of *the Kitchen Sisters* from Herbert, selling Aloe Vera to sunburned tourists on the beach in Jamaica, and heard on *Something Understood: the Singing Manifesto* a Falling Tree production for BBC Radio 4, Jan 2009; **Sleep, Sleep, Little One Sleep** Traditional Japanese, from the Edo era – 17th to 19th Century. From Keishi Nagatsuka. translation KH 2010; **Ja-Janka** Traditional Korean. From Sunghee Yu and her mother and grandmother. English version KH 2010; **All the Pretty Little Horses** Traditional American. Many sources; **Sleep Johnny Sleep** Traditional Czech. Czech words in *Lullabies from the Cradle*, Languages from the Cradle Partnership, EU project. English version KH 2010; **Go to Bed Tom** Traditional English, known to the author from childhood; **The Sun Goes Down** Traditional Austrian. In Volksmusik in Tirol, Band 3, Insbruck 1986. English version KH 2010; **Bedtime Aunties** Traditional Bangla. From Mr Allama Siddiki, Deputy High Commissioner, Bangladesh HC, London and his wife and colleagues. English version KH 2010; **Not Luisa!** Traditional Italian. From Edda Peris and her mother Armida Sgnaolin. English version KH 2010; **Sleep Come Quickly** Traditional French, from the Auvergne. Several sources. English version KH 2010; **Hushabye Baby Hush** Traditional Russian. From Jim Riordan and Yelena Pershina with thanks. This English version KH 2010; **Ninna Nanna** Traditional Italian. Several oral sources. English version KH 2010; **Tutu Maramba** Traditional lullaby from Brazil. English version KH 2010; **Sleep Baby Sleep** Traditional Hungarian. Hungarian words and music in Cass-Beggs *Folk Lullabies*, Oak, 1969. English version KH 2010; **La-La-La Lai** Traditional Iranian. From Zohreh Korangi, via Phillippa Clayden. Hear it on YouTube. **Maranoa lullaby** A Murri song from the Aborigines of Queensland, collected by Dr H O Lethbridge, adapted by Mark Leehy and Kevin O'Mara, in *Moondrops*, Moondrake Australia, 1993; **Great Grandmother's Lullaby** Traditional Korean. From Sunghee Yu's mother, Byungyun Kim, who had it from her grandmother. English version KH 2010; **The Sun Sleeps** Traditional Greek. From *The Folklore of Chios*, Vol 2, Philip P Argenti and H J Rose, Cambridge University Press, 1949

nei

la la la lai

ninna nanna

eili liuli

laylay

liuli lulu li

neeni

ninna nanna djo-djo alulu

ninnice

ooo ooo ooo ooo

thoi thoi thoi

su su su su

arruru arrurruru

azeri